IMAGES
of America

LOST
IDORA PARK

As automobile traffic increased, Idora Park opened a second entrance and expanded the south parking lot. This new entrance cut through the adjoining neighborhood south of the park and intersected with Canfield Road. The new road was named Billingsgate on June 29, 1929, for manager and part owner Rex Billings. The Jack Rabbit roller coaster (left) was a welcoming first sight for park-goers. (Courtesy of Bob Dyce.)

ON THE COVER: The Wildcat consisted of three trains of five cars each. In 1940, the Wildcat's "aeroplane curve" had to be altered because it was so severe that "women fainted and children were afraid to ride." The ride was too fast to run all three trains safely, so only two trains could be run at the same time. (Courtesy of Walter Menning.)

Published by Arcadia Publishing
Charleston, South Carolina

Library of Congress Control Number: 2019935414

For all general information, please contact Arcadia Publishing:
Telephone 843-853-2070
Fax 843-853-0044
E-mail sales@arcadiapublishing.com
For customer service and orders:
Toll-Free 1-888-313-2665

Visit us on the Internet at www.arcadiapublishing.com

To the memory of Richard L. Amey. You saved our family.

The Silver Rocket Ships (left) arrived in 1948 and anchored the upper midway. Three rockets were suspended from an 85-foot tower. Circling above park-goers, the rockets each had four rows of seats, allowing up to 12 riders. There were no seatbelts. The Rocket Lunching Pad, located beneath the ride, offered refreshment booths. Idora Park's Famous French Fries booth can be seen in the background. (Courtesy of Jim Pruchniewicz.)

IMAGES
of America

LOST
IDORA PARK

James M. Amey and Toni L. Amey
of The Idora Park Experience

ARCADIA
PUBLISHING

CONTENTS

ACKNOWLEDGMENTS

Our deepest gratitude to Rich Amey and Linda Williams, who taught us that sometimes, rescuing something that has been abandoned can make something great happen. To our children, thank you for trying to understand the insanity that is The Idora Park Experience and for not asking why we spent your inheritance on a museum.

Thank you to four of the best friends ever, Marie and Tony Coyne, who traveled 3,600 miles to make sure the show went on, and Larry and Linda Cadman, who are always there for us—especially when the museum is opening.

To Rick and Jodie Amey, Bill and Jean Amey, Tim and Leann Groves, Nick and Patty DePinto, John Kost, and Dana Eyer, thank you for your love and support and for working tirelessly for the meager wages of a sandwich and cold drink. To Lenny Cavalier, Rick Shale, Matt and Dawn Schwartz, Dave Price, Mike Brocious, Bill Lawson and the staff of the Mahoning Valley Historical Society, thank you for sharing your knowledge.

To all the fans of The Idora Park Experience, this is your story. And to Stan Boney and Lorie Quigley Barber, thank you for making us understand the importance of telling this story.

Many of the images in this volume are courtesy of The Idora Park Experience (TIPE), most of which have been donated. Many came directly from the owner, as is the case with donations from Frances Antijunti (Antijunti), Kathy Carnahan (Carnahan), the Doll family (Doll), Bill Eynon (Eynon), Nancy Filkorn (Filkorn), Jessica Garland (Garland), Russell Hardy (Hardy), Michael Jenkins (Jenkins), Jack and Sally Kenney (Kenney), Nancy McKinney (McKinney), Carol Morris (Morris), Lorne Mossman (Mossman), Jim Olson (Olson), Stella and Jim Parks (Parks), Jim Pruchniewicz (Pruchniewicz), Dianne Reedy (Reedy), Orville Ritchie (Ritchie), Mike Roncone (Roncone), Matt and Dawn Schwartz (Schwartz), and Fred Shepherd (Shepherd). Bob Dyce (Dyce) also donated several original photograph slides and granted permission for the use of many others of which he retains ownership.

A few collections have been donated by the heirs, as is the case with the images from the Don Maffitt Sr. collection (Maffitt), which was donated by his children Denise Connor, Donnie Maffitt Jr., and Doreen White; the Walter Menning collection (Menning), which was donated by Dave and Stephanie Dangerfield; and the Youngstown Slag collection, which was donated by John Mulichak (Mulichak).

There are also images courtesy of Bill Amey (Amey), Tammi Anderson (Anderson), Janet Eiler (Eiler), Laurie Burns Fox (Fox), David Goddard (Goddard), Lori Nard in honor of her husband Dick Nard (Nard), Eric Sakowski (Sakowski), Cheryl Thompson-Morrow (Thompson-Morrow), Michele Horvath Toth (Toth), Janet Yosay (Yosay), and James and Karen Zagorsky (Zagorsky).

And finally, the Lenny Cavalier collection is courtesy of the Mahoning Valley Historical Society in Youngstown, Ohio (MVHS).

INTRODUCTION

Most everyone who experienced Idora Park had a love-hate relationship with the amusement park. They loved it while they had it and hated it when it left.

It started out as a small picnic area at the end of a trolley line on the relatively unpopulated south side of Youngstown, Ohio. The original name for the new park was Terminal Park, appropriately named since it sat at the end, or terminus, of the trolley line.

The name changed in 1899 to Idora Park. There are at least a dozen theories as to how the name came about. They range from a shortened version of "I Adore A Park," to the name of a girl or woman who once lived in the area, to a competition for the town's favorite school teacher, who would get to choose the new name for the park. Somehow, the teacher who came in second place, and not the winner, received this honor, if this particular theory is true. Another popular idea attributes the name to a tribe of Indians who once inhabited the area. The problem with this is that there is no evidence of a tribe named Idora anywhere near Youngstown. So, how Idora truly got its name is a mystery, but historians continue to search for the answer.

Idora Park grew quickly in size and popularity. The little seven-acre picnic grounds expanded to slightly more than 26 acres as surrounding plots were acquired over the coming years.

Early attractions included a carousel pavilion, a casino, a theater, and the first roller coaster, then later, a huge ballroom, a funhouse, a Ferris wheel, bowling, billiards, roller skating, more roller coasters, a water ride, the first caterpillar ride, Skee-Ball, a giant swimming pool, bumper cars, and then the coup de grace, the king of the midway—the Wildcat roller coaster. It arrived in 1930 along with a new water ride, the Rapids. Miniature golf was built the same year. Later, a large rocket ship ride arrived, then a turtle ride, and more, always growing and always improving. The swimming pool closed and was filled in, and a Kiddieland opened on its former site.

Owners and managers came and went, as did World War I, the Great Depression, World War II, the Korean War, the Vietnam War, and the civil rights riots; Idora Park survived it all and actually thrived. Yes, there were minor setbacks and some tragedies. Accidents occurred; most were minor, some serious, and several resulted in death. At least four people drowned in the pool, three people were killed on roller coasters, and one employee was shot and killed while working his booth. On one occasion, as if in some scene from an old movie, there was even a robbery with safecrackers who managed to tie up the night watchman and open the park's five safes, making off with about $20,000.

Idora Park grew with the local community. Youngstown had high employment and good jobs. But cracks started to appear when the steel mills started closing and laying off workers. These were big cracks. Thousands of people were out of work, and many found it necessary to leave town for employment elsewhere. The population was dwindling, and so were the crowds going to Idora Park.

Company picnics, which had been an important staple in Idora's revenue stream, began tapering off with the closing of the mills and the companies that supported them. It was a vicious cycle, but the park's owners came up with new ideas to get people into the parks. A pay-as-you-enter pricing plan that had been started a decade earlier was expanded so that anyone coming into the park was paying to be there. This helped eliminate loiterers. Efforts continued to book the best local and national talent at the ballroom. Idora was treading water, but just barely.

The park was put up for sale in 1982 for $1.5 million, but there were no takers. The owners vowed to stay open, and the park opened again the following year and prepared for the year after that.

Idora suffered several fires in its history. There was a fire on the midway in 1951 that destroyed almost $25,000 worth of property, and a 1957 fire that caused $5,000 worth of damage in Kiddieland. But nothing like the fire of April 26, 1984, had ever happened at the park. A worker using a torch in the Lost River ride left for his lunch break at his home in the neighborhood that bordered Idora. His friend and coworker joined him.

In a short while, the men heard sirens approaching and then passing the house. As they looked outside, they saw that fire trucks were headed into Idora Park. The large plume of black smoke rising from the park appeared to be coming from the area where the welder had been working prior to his lunch break. As they watched the billowing smoke, the reality of what was happening began to set in, and the welder's friend later recalled his words: "I think I just burned down Idora Park."

The park could not recover from the fire. At the end of the season, it closed for good. In October 1984, a two-day auction dispersed the treasures of Idora Park far and wide.

In 1976, James M. "Jim" Amey worked at Idora Park. At the end of that summer, he joined the military and was stationed overseas when the park burned. It had little effect on him at the time. It would be another nine years before he realized the devastation. In the winter of 1993, he and his soon-to-be wife, Toni, walked through the park. Toni, who grew up in California, had never seen Idora Park. Needless to say, her first visit did not live up to the expectations Jim's stories had set up.

For Jim, the realization that Idora Park was truly gone became shockingly apparent by the deterioration of the buildings still standing and those in ruins on the ground. While walking toward the Arcade building, a sensation not unlike déjà vu was felt. Jim saw the remains of the Football Throw game booth he had worked 17 years prior. Hanging from the booth's rotting façade was a porcelain light socket barely holding on by one rusty screw. That porcelain light socket was not going to be left to disappear, as Idora Park seem doomed to do. Jim took that light socket and started something that would grow into a passion—finding whatever else might remain of Idora Park.

The dream would take 20 more years before it became a reality, but 30 years to the day that Idora Park burned, The Idora Park Experience rose from those ashes.

Authors Toni and Jim Amey sit in the 20-foot-long 1948 Rocket Ship at The Idora Park Experience museum in Canfield, Ohio. After many years of searching, the Ameys have amassed a huge collection of artifacts from Idora Park. The Ameys open the museum to the public twice a year. (Photograph by Tim Groves.)

One

THE THRILL OF AN
85-YEAR LOVE AFFAIR

This two-sided "Idora Park" neon sign on Parkview Avenue greeted trolley riders and, later, travelers by automobile and bus to the park. The Parkview entrance underwent several changes through the years, including the expansion of a parking lot and the addition of a sheltered bus stop. This restored sign is located in the Youngstown Historical Center of Industry and Labor. (Yosay.)

This trolley scroll came from one of the early Youngstown Park and Falls streetcars that carried crowds to Idora Park. Traveling by streetcar was by far the primary method of transportation from the park's opening into the 1910s, when automobile ownership was increasing and more people started driving themselves to the park. Conveniently, or maybe coincidentally, a new viaduct was completed on Market Street in 1899, just one week before Idora Park opened to the public. The viaduct, brainchild of the streetcar's directors, was a bridge that joined downtown Youngstown to the city's south side and, of course, provided better access to Idora Park. Streetcars, automobiles, foot traffic, and animal cart traffic could now cross safely above the hills, ravines, river, and railroad tracks that had once inhibited travel and presented so many hazards. The viaduct also opened up opportunities for the development of Youngstown's south side for businesses and new homes. This trolley scroll is on display at The Idora Park Experience. (TIPE.)

Streetcar passengers disembark for a day at Idora Park in this image, titled "Arrival At Park," from the souvenir booklet *Idora and Mill Creek Park, Season of 1901.* Idora Park's second season, 1900, was more successful than the first. Attendance for 1900 doubled 1899's numbers. (TIPE.)

This postcard shows the streetcar line as it curves southeast to its stop near the front of the ornate ballroom in the background, facing west (left). In 1910, management chose the southernmost end of the park as the location for the huge new ballroom, and wisely extended the trolley line for easier access by patrons who wanted to dance. (TIPE.)

In this 1927 photograph, patrons arriving from the streetcars find themselves at the south end of the lower midway and facing the front of the ballroom (right). The Firefly Figure-Eight roller coaster (left) was built in 1920 and was demolished in 1929 to make way for a new water ride and a new coaster. (Mulichak.)

Parkview Avenue parking lots, located at the north end of Idora Park, were expanded over the years as more and more automobiles arrived. A corrugated, curved-roof bus shelter and stop (right) was added. Idora Park bought the large eagle seen in this May 1949 photograph from the Great Lakes Exposition in Cleveland. (Olson.)

It is summer in 1945, and standing at the Billingsgate Road entrance with the day's treasure, including a face-sticking candy apple, are five-year-old Jozy Burns and her brother, three-year-old Tom Burns. The siblings have just enjoyed a fun-filled day at Idora Park and are heading home with their mother, Mary Burns, who stopped to snap this photograph. The triangular signage and lighted US flag atop the stone structure include two Idora Park neon signs to welcome park-goers arriving on Billingsgate Road from Canfield Road. A big "Thank You" bids farewell. The stone structure and signage was likely erected in 1925 when the Billingsgate entrance opened at the south end of the park. The structure is known to have remained in place at least until 1951. This pair of neon signs sold at auction on October 20, 1984, for $175. One of the restored signs is at The Idora Park Experience. (Fox.)

This large metal sign replaced the stone structure on Billingsgate Road as early as 1952, and remained in place until well after Idora Park closed in 1984. Both sides contained a series of yellow chaser lights that flashed sequentially, racing toward the end and a lighted "exploding" star. The sequence repeated continuously. The new sign included a marquee to advertise events. (Zagorsky.)

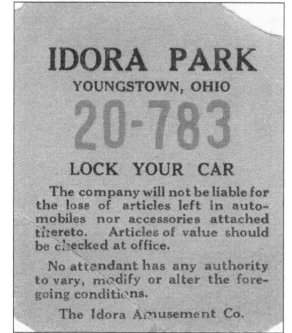

After turning onto Billingsgate Road from Canfield Road, a short drive along the median-divided road brought visitors to a stone gatehouse where two park employees collected 25¢ per vehicle for parking. Drivers were handed a parking permit and then proceeded toward the Billingsgate parking lot. (Shepherd.)

The Jack Rabbit roller coaster comes into view on the right. Screaming and laughter are heard as one of the coaster trains races past. One can only imagine the thoughts going through their minds as siblings Tom and Jozy Burns hold hands in this 1945 photograph and look up in wonder at the huge wooden structure before them. A narrow strip of ground and a short wooden fence were all that separated the Jack Rabbit from the parking lot. Only two trains ran on the Jack Rabbit, each with three cars. The cars had three rows of seats and were wide enough to accommodate up to three passengers per row. There were no individual restraints; one long pair of leather seatbelts ran the length of the seats and was shared by all in that row. (Fox.)

The ornate ballroom, pictured above in 1927, opened to the public on June 20, 1910, replacing the casino that was built in 1899 as the primary dance hall. The ballroom was originally built with open sides to allow fresh air to circulate inside the building. Several renovations took place over the following years. Canvas sides were added to block inclement weather, and heating was installed to allow dancing throughout the year. Eventually, solid walls enclosed the sides of the structure. The decorative cupolas and towers and much of the façade were removed in 1955 and 1956, leaving a plain, flatter roofline. Below, longtime park employee Walter Menning can be seen under the oak tree at right, directly in front of his "Fool the Guesser" weight scale. (Above, Mulichak; below, Jenkins.)

Many big-name performers, as well as local legends, were headliners at the ballroom. In 1960, the dance schedule included Glenn Miller for Wednesday, June 29. This would have been the Glenn Miller Band and not Glenn Miller himself, as Miller had disappeared in December 1944 during World War II. In the years prior to and after 1960, the Idora Park Ballroom hosted popular performers including comedians, singers, and music from jazz, polka, country, and rock-n-roll bands. Many visitors to the museum tell stories about meeting their spouse at one of Idora's dances or how their parents or grandparents met during one of the ballroom events, and how had it not been for Idora Park, that person might never have been born. (Both, Filkorn.)

Beautiful

IDORA PARK

presents

SUMMER DANCING SCHEDULE

★

1960

Sunday, May 8—Harry James	Saturday, July 16—Bobby Dale
Saturday, May 14—Tommy Carlyn	Wednesday, July 20—Peter Palmer
Wednesday, May 18—Stan Kenton	Saturday, July 23—Johnny Murphy
Saturday, May 21—Artie Arnell	Wednesday, July 27—Les Brown
Saturday, May 28—Buddy Lee	Saturday, July 30—Lee Barrett
Saturday, June 4—Guy Lombardo	Wednesday, August 3—Sammy Kaye
Saturday, June 11—Tommy Carlyn	Saturday, August 6—Tommy Carlyn
Wednesday, June 15—Maynard Ferguson and Dave Brubek	Wednesday, August 10—Four Freshmen
Saturday, June 18—Artie Arnell	Saturday, August 13—Artie Arnell
Wednesday, June 22—Billy May	Wednesday, August 17—Buddy Morrow
Saturday, June 25—Russ Romero	Saturday, August 20—Hal Curtis
Wednesday, June 29—Glenn Miller	Wednesday, August 24—Clyde McCoy
Saturday, July 2—Tommy Carlyn	Saturday, August 27—Bobby Dale
Wednesday, July 6—Dukes of Dixieland	Wednesday, August 31—To be announced later
Saturday, July 9—Artie Arnell	
Wednesday, July 13—Louis Armstrong	Saturday, September 3—Russ Romero

The 18-hole miniature golf course made its debut in 1930 as the 19th Hole on the west side of the lower midway. In 1964, the course underwent a $25,000 renovation that included a neon sign added to the roof of the building and changes to four of the holes. Groups were limited to a maximum of four players. Players received a scorecard with a list of rules and a pencil for keeping score. The course featured six holes that were par two, eleven holes that were par three, and one par-four hole. Par for the first nine was 25 strokes, and par for the second nine was 24 strokes, making this a par 49 course. (Above, Nard; below, TIPE.)

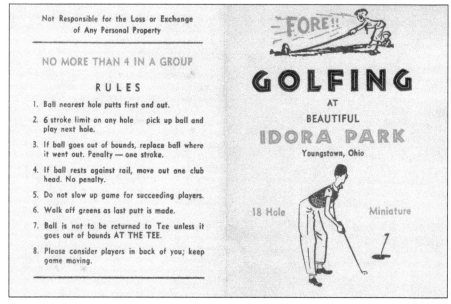

Not Responsible for the Loss or Exchange of Any Personal Property

NO MORE THAN 4 IN A GROUP

RULES

1. Ball nearest hole putts first and out.

2. 6 stroke limit on any hole — pick up ball and play next hole.

3. If ball goes out of bounds, replace ball where it went out. Penalty — one stroke.

4. If ball rests against rail, move out one club head. No penalty.

5. Do not slow up game for succeeding players.

6. Walk off greens as last putt is made.

7. Ball is not to be returned to Tee unless it goes out of bounds AT THE TEE.

8. Please consider players in back of you; keep game moving.

FORE!!

GOLFING

AT

BEAUTIFUL

IDORA PARK

Youngstown, Ohio

18 Hole   Miniature

Management took advantage of the fact that the words *bingo* and *Idora* had the same number of letters, so playing cards were labeled with the *Idora* name. The rules were the same as bingo. Players could purchase any number of Idora playing cards for 10¢ per card and play their own plastic chips to cover the called numbers, or they could use the extra-large kernels of corn that were supplied by the park for that purpose. Tim Hardy, who called the Idora game for several years, said that often, players would buy more cards than they could manage and not be able to keep up with his number calling. Occasionally, frustrated players would throw kernels of corn at him in an effort to make him slow down. (Above, Menning; below, TIPE.)

I	D	O	R	A
3496				
12	23	35	56	70
3	18	31	58	63
15	25	FREE	51	71
6	19	33	49	65
7	26	36	47	66

Monkey Island opened in 1928 as a small building on a man-made island. A low perimeter wall surrounded the island to prevent the monkeys from escaping. More than 50 monkeys arrived for 1928, and they quickly became the most popular animal attraction at the park. Animals were an important feature in the park's early years through the late 1940s. A pony track was relocated several times as Idora Park acquired adjoining plots of land and expanded. Idora also had a zoo with deer, bears, and at least one wildcat. Tragically, 11-year-old Velma Lewis was attacked and injured by one of the bears as she fed it acorns through its cage. One hand was partially amputated, and her entire scalp was ripped from her head. Her family sued and was awarded $7,500. At one point, a wildcat escaped from the zoo, but the event was kept quiet, and no media reports have been found of the animal's final disposition. (TIPE.)

Monkeys and baboons were a popular attraction at Idora Park for two decades. On Three-Cent Kiddies' Day in 1929, the park opened early at 5:30 a.m. to huge crowds. Several boys made their way into Monkey Island to sneak off with the monkeys, but they were caught. The great monkey escape of August 24, 1947, saw more than two dozen monkeys escape. Some headed for nearby Mill Creek Park, while others climbed atop Idora's buildings and refused to come down. A few were recaptured, several became vicious and had to be put down, and many were never found. By the end of the 1949 season, the remaining monkeys and baboons were sold off for $25 each. (Both, Toth.)

Roller-skating arrived at Idora in 1910 or possibly 1904. In 1915, roller-skating left a building that then became the dining facility. A roller-skating building was erected in 1916 at the northeast end of the park, but in 1921, roller-skating returned to the earlier dining facility location. In 1931, the Funhouse was converted into a roller-skating rink. Confusion reigns until 1938, when the ballroom began hosting night skating. In 1939, as the photograph above shows, a fenced, outdoor roller-skating rink was constructed on the upper midway. Indoor evening skating returned to the ballroom at the end of each dance season. Skaters could purchase merchandise like the cloth patch at left. (Above, Antijunti, left, TIPE.)

The photography gallery was a long-standing operation on the midway, beginning in 1910. Charles D. Hoover was an artist and photographer who owned a studio in Youngstown as well as the Idora Park gallery. His family ran the business at Idora for 40 years, drawing caricatures and taking photographs. Patrons could dress up and pose in various getups and buy three photographs for 10¢. As a young couple, author Jim Amey's grandparents Leona Mae and Louis H. "Bud" Amey posed in the Idora Park photography booth; decades later, they posed again. (Both, Amey.)

By 1924, Youngstown's population was growing rapidly, but only two municipal pools existed. Building a pool at Idora Park made good financial sense. Ground was broken in the northeast corner of the upper midway for the $100,000 swimming pool, semi-circular dressing room, and a water filtration plant. The swimming pool was oval, measuring 210 feet by 160 feet and 10.5 feet at its deepest. (Mulichak.)

Tragically, there were at least four recorded drownings in the pool. Three were children who drowned within a three-week span in 1944. The 1944 drownings include a 13-year-old boy in late May and two drownings in mid-June on the same day involving sisters aged 13 and 12. The girls' bodies were not found until the next day. (Mulichak.)

This postcard bears the 1923 marketing slogan "Beautiful Idora Park," although the swimming pool opened a year later, in 1924. The pool water was touted as "clean enough to drink" thanks to the filtration system that circulated and cleaned the water daily. In 1939, however, management ordered that a new well be drilled, and a saltwater aquifer was found, thus converting the pool for saltwater swimming. (TIPE.)

On August 5, 1930, bandleader Ace Brigode takes time out from performing in the Idora Park Ballroom with his band, Ace Brigode and his Fourteen Virginians, to visit the swimming pool. Built by the Heller-Murray Construction Company of Youngstown, the pool included a 20-foot-wide sandy beach. Daredevil diving acts and a bathing beauty contest were also held at the pool. (Thompson-Morrow.)

The Baby Wildcat coaster (left), as it would come to be known, built in 1934, was relocated twice. Its final location was behind the ladies' restroom, the four stone-pillar building with three roof dormers in the background at right. The swimming pool, to the right of the ladies' restroom, closed in 1949 and reopened as Motor Boat Lagoon, featuring gasoline-powered boats on a circular route. Motor Boat Lagoon closed after its second season when a worker was badly burned. Fuel vapors ignited while he was refueling one of the boats. In 1951, the swimming pool was completely filled in, and Kiddieland was built overtop it. (Jenkins.)

This view of the upper midway facing northwest, near the Parkview Avenue entrance, shows the roller-skating rink (left), which was moved in 1931 into the old Funhouse building. From the late 1930s into the 1940s, Playland was a small version of the Kiddieland that would be built in 1951. The baby boom was in full swing after World War II, and many young couples brought their children to the park. By the late 1940s, management saw the revenue potential in expanding the children's play area, but a suitable spot was needed. Swimming pool drownings, competition from new city pools, and the severely burned employee at Motor Boat Lagoon were considerations for closing the pool. Below, children ride the Baby Wildcat in 1962. (Above, Jenkins; below, Toth.)

In 1908, the drinking fountains received cooling devices, which is likely what caused the change from cylindrical to a more hourglass shape. There were two stone water fountains, and each had four separate Halsey-Taylor porcelain bowls with four bubblers. The water fountains were located on the lower midway in front of the Wildcat and in the upper midway near the Tilt-A-Whirl. (Schwartz.)

A Porky the Paper Eater in a mushroom house, two Porkys in small shed-like houses, and two Leo the lions in shed-type cages arrived in the mid-1960s. Recordings asked park-goers for paper "food." A suction device pulled the paper into the creature's mouth. The mushroom Porky sold for $625 at auction and the others sold for $525 each. (Zagorsky.)

Two nutcracker soldiers guarded the entrance to Kiddieland on the site of what once was the swimming pool from 1925 to 1949 and then the Motor Boat Lagoon from 1949 to 1950. The semi-circular bathhouse remained in place and was used as a picnic area. The Baby Wildcat roller coaster was just outside this area, at far left behind the ladies' restroom. The other 14 children's rides were located within Kiddieland and included the Allan Herschell G-12 Miniature Train No.

419, Allan Herschell Skyfighter, Allan Herschell Wet Boat, Pinto Fire Engine, Allan Herschell Kiddie Buggy ride, Ihle Mercedes Cars, Hampton Tubs of Fun, Hampton Dry Boat, Mangels Kiddie Carousel, Mangels Kiddie Whip, Bulgey the Whale, Hobby Horse Merry-Go-Round, the Jet Swing, and the Chance Kiddie Turtle. (Nard.)

Three-year-old Billy Amey relaxes while riding the Kiddieland wooden airplane swing ride in July 1951, right before his fourth birthday in August. The wooden airplanes were eventually replaced with metal jet planes that had been converted from war surplus airplane fuel tanks. Bud and Mae Amey took their four children—Marilyn, Rich, Bob, and Billy—to Idora Park once each year to celebrate the youngsters' birthdays. This was the first summer Kiddieland was in the former swimming pool and Motor Boat Lagoon location. Below, Billy Amey rides the Hobby Horse merry-go-round. (Both, Amey.)

This Allan Herschell Kiddie Buggy ride was made in New York. The pony is cast aluminum, and the cart is wood. The ride was sold at the Idora Park auction in 1984 for $3,000, but was mistakenly listed by the auctioneers as a Pinto Brothers Pony Cart. (Eiler.)

The Gebr Ihle Mercedes-Benz cars arrived in 1966. They were built in Germany and were based on the full-sized 1955 Mercedes-Benz SL 300. They were powered by an electric motor in the trunk. Here, Mark Amey seems to be enjoying the ride. (TIPE.)

The Allan Herschell wet boat ride was a favorite Kiddieland ride. The boats did not have their own motors; they were attached to a metal pole that held them in position as they floated counter-clockwise within a 25-foot circular water trough. Did the kids know they were not actually steering the boats? (Maffitt.)

American patriotism was always present at Idora. In 1976, America's bicentennial year, many of the buildings and rides were painted red, white, and blue, especially anything that remotely resembled military equipment, like this Sky Fighter ride, complete with guns that made a machine-gun sound when the trigger was squeezed. (Nard.)

This Turtle ride was the smaller, kiddie version of Idora Park's full-size Turtle ride. Both were created by the R.E. Chambers Engineering Company in Beaver Falls, Pennsylvania, and were based on the earlier Tumble Bug design. The three kiddie turtles traveled up and down small hills on a circular track. The Turtle sold for $4,500 at auction. (Zagorsky.)

Kiddieland had this smaller version of the adult-sized whip ride. The W.F. Mangels Kiddie Whip arrived sometime after Kiddieland opened in 1951, but its history is vague. It is known that the ride remained until the park's closure in 1984, and it sold for $1,500 at auction. (Zagorsky.)

This metal jet airplane swing ride replaced the old Kiddieland wooden planes. Inclement weather and wear and tear from daily use took their toll on the wooden planes. They did not look much like airplanes anyway, since they had no propeller or wings. Management felt that it was time to upgrade. Few new rides had been built through the mid-1940s because of rationing for the war effort. After World War II, surplus war materials were made available to the public in government-run auctions. Creative-thinking amusement-ride makers bought whatever military generators, motors, vehicles, and other useful materials they could get their hands on. Military aircraft wing fuel tanks and belly fuel tanks were sleek and streamlined and could be used, after some modifications, to create many different types of rides and attractions. In the 1950s, the public, especially kids, were fascinated with rockets and jets. (Toth.)

This Allan Herschell
G12 kiddie train No. 419
arrived at the park in 1951.
It consisted of a power car
operated by an "engineer"
operator, two passenger cars,
and one observation car, for
a total of three passenger
cars that could seat up to
14 children. The train was
named the *Idora Special*. It
traveled on a 12-inch-gauge
steel track that was laid in
an oval shape around a large
garden within Kiddieland.
Ride operators disliked the
kiddie train more than any
other ride, especially on hot
summer days, which brought
forth screams of pain
when little kiddie bottoms
sat on the scorching hot
metal seats. (Both, Eiler.)

A rainy day does not stop the smiles on these children's faces as they ride the Kiddieland fire trucks. The ride was built by the Pinto Brothers of Coney Island, New York, which made many different kiddie rides in the 1940s and 1950s. It sold at auction for $3,000. (Dyce.)

The Tubs-O-Fun was a new ride created in 1953 by the Hampton Amusement Company. Idora received theirs that same year. An electric motor turned six arms in a circle. The end of each arm was attached to a single tub. The riders could spin their tub by turning the wheel mounted in the center. (Nard.)

The Idora Park Hook and Ladder Fire Truck arrived in 1951. It was a 1948 Crosley pickup truck conversion with the bed removed. The remaining cab served as the "tractor," powered by a four-cylinder engine. A specially fabricated trailer carried the children. Ladders that ran the length of the trailer were on hinges, and served as safety restraints that folded into the children's laps to keep them in their seats. Depending on the varying size of the riders, the hook and ladder could usually seat 20 children comfortably. Overland Amusement Company in Maine was the only company to build Crosley hook-and-ladder fire trucks, and it is believed only four of them were built. Idora Park's hook-and-ladder truck is considered to be the most rare of the four vehicles. Its last confirmed location was in 2011, in restored condition in Missouri. (Parks.)

Some style or other of a children's automobile ride had been at the park since the mid-1930s and was always placed in a location near or in the children's play areas. The style seen here, driven along a fixed wooden track by Bob and Shelly Horvath in 1962, arrived that same year. (Toth.)

Idora Park's gem, the full-size carousel that arrived in 1922 and now resides in New York City, received all of the attention from the media. This beautiful W.F. Mangels Kiddie Carousel is, unfortunately, largely forgotten. The carousel had 24 horses in three rows of eight and two chariots. The ride sold for $6,250 at auction. (Dyce.)

40

These Hampton dry boats floated on tires, not water. Two tires mounted under the boats followed a circular track with hills and valleys. The boats could hold six passengers. Each was brightly painted and had three rows of seats with two nonfunctioning steering wheels per row. Two mock Mercury outboard motors were mounted at the rear of each boat. (Dyce.)

This postcard presents a partial view of many of Kiddieland's rides and the semi-circular building in the background that was built in 1924 as the swimming pool bathhouse, which was converted to a picnic area when Kiddieland was erected over the pool in 1951. The *Idora Limited* train in the foreground followed a scenic route throughout beautiful Idora Park. (TIPE.)

This *C.P. Huntington* locomotive, built by Chance Manufacturing, arrived in 1964, replacing the National Amusement Device's gasoline-engine-powered, six-car passenger train that had been at Idora since 1937. Both trains were known as the *Idora Limited*. The *C.P. Huntington* followed the same two-foot gauge track as the old train, and retained the same train station, which was located in the upper midway near the French fry stand. The *C.P. Huntington* was gasoline powered and pulled four open passenger cars, each with a canvas roof. The train and tracks sold at auction upon Idora Park's closure. The winning bid was $28,500. The train is currently functioning at Pymatuning Deer Park in Pennsylvania. (Above, Dyce; below, Nard.)

The lower midway began once park-goers were inside the ticketing entrance at the southwest end of the ballroom. This photograph from 1974 or 1975 shows, from left to right in the background, the south parking area, the Eyerly Spider ride, and the Chance Turbo ride. The swings of the Chance YoYo ride can be seen at top right. (Maffitt.)

The Chance Turbo ride occupied two different locations. First, it was on the lower midway from 1971 to 1973, as seen here. Then, in 1974, the Turbo was moved to the farthest spot on the lower midway, closer to the ballroom. The Turbo was gone before the 1976 season. (MVHS.)

The carousel was one of several favorite places to take a break or meet up with family or friends on the lower midway, as seen here in August 1958. Children who had been out enjoying the park's rides, games, attractions, and food could check in with their parents before heading out for more adventure. (Menning.)

The first carousel building was built on the upper midway in 1898, but was destroyed in a fire in 1909. A new carousel building replaced it on the lower midway. That building survived the fire of April 26, 1984, thanks to the dedicated fire crews who concentrated their efforts on saving the 1922 carousel within. (Nard.)

The third full-sized carousel arrived in 1922. It occupied the second carousel pavilion built at Idora. This new carousel was built by the Philadelphia Toboggan Company of Pennsylvania and was designated PTC No. 61. It consisted of 48 horses in three rows: 30 horses were full-size, 18 were ponies, and there were two chariots. All 48 horses were hand carved by Daniel Muller and painted by Gustav Weiss. The Dentzel carousel that had occupied the pavilion since 1911 was sold to Cascade Park in New Castle, Pennsylvania, for $1,000. (Above, Mossman; below, Zagorsky.)

Arrow Development Company formed in California in 1946. By 1964, Arrow had designed and built open-topped antique cars that resembled Ford Model Ts. The cars were five-eighths the size of the full-size Ford Model T touring car, had a front seat and a rear seat, and could fit five people. A single pedal on the floor near the driver's feet served as both the accelerator and the brake. When the pedal was depressed, the car would accelerate. When it was released, the car would slow and stop. A control pedal was located on the right front running board should an attending employee need to control a car that was being mishandled. However, the track and guide mechanism was such that the car maintained a set course, and the operator had very little control over steering. A one-cylinder gasoline engine supplied power to the rear axle by way of a system of belt pulleys and chain sprockets. The car was capable of reaching a top speed of four miles per hour. (Maffitt.)

Soon after the Arrow cars arrived in 1969, Idora's three owners met to discuss naming the new ride, but could not come up with something that was catchy. Lenny Cavalier, part owner of Idora Park, went home that day and described the ride to Mary, his wife. She recalled two popular television programs, *Petticoat Junction* and *Green Acres*, that were set in or near the fictional town of Hooterville, and suggested the ride be called Hooterville Highway. Lenny did not like the name and told her so. But the next day, he mentioned her suggestion to his two partners, who loved it. The rest is, as they say, history. (Both, Nard.)

The Flying Cages arrived in 1962. Mastering this ride involved the rider shifting their body weight from one side of the cage to the other to get it to swing back and forth in increasing arcs until it went over the top in a complete circle. Just getting it started took quite a bit of energy. The rider was continuously running, throwing their weight against one side of the cage, then turning and running to do the same to the opposite side. It was common to lose footing and crash face first into the inside of the cage. The chance of getting hurt was increased when two people were in one cage, or if the riders were impaired by alcohol. (Zagorsky.)

In 1949, Lusse Brothers bumper cars were purchased. A new building to house the ride went up at the north end of the upper midway and remained in that location throughout the park's history. The attraction was named Auto Skooter. Power to the cars came from a steel grid in the ceiling and contacts under the cars that touched the steel floor. A pole called a "stinger" was mounted at the rear of the car and came in contact with the ceiling, completing the electrical circuit that powered the car. In 1971, the ride was renamed Helter Skelter, and the cars no longer had to travel in one direction but could bump in any direction. Duce bumper cars were imported for the change. (Right, Eiler; below, Zagorsky.)

The Turtle was a modified Tumble Bug ride that was built by the R.E. Chambers Company in Beaver Falls, Pennsylvania. The primary difference between the Turtle and the Tumble Bug was the ride's head. The Turtle had a large turtle head, while the Tumble Bug had a flat disk. A Tumble Bug did arrive at Idora in 1941, but no record was found indicating when or why it left. However, the Turtle ride arrived in 1954. The five Turtle cars each had an electric motor that propelled them around a 100-foot-diameter, hill-and-valley single-rail track. A sixth Turtle car was held in reserve. (Above, Nard; below, Maffitt.)

Herbert Sellner invented the Tilt-A-Whirl in 1926 after experimenting with different designs in his backyard, using chairs from his kitchen. Idora's first Tilt-A-Whirl arrived in 1928. The ride consisted of seven open-faced, curved cars that could accommodate three or more riders, depending on the size of the riders. The footwell at the front of each car had a pivot point that was secured to the ride's base platform. This pivot point and two fixed caster wheels under the frame allowed the car to spin freely in a 360-degree arc. A U-shaped metal safety bar locked in place to help secure the riders and allow them some control over their movement. The platform moved in a circle with undulating bumps. The cars would spin in varying speeds and direction, depending upon the weight in the car, combined with the platform rotation. Various models of the ride would come and go. The ride was often called the "Tilt-A-Hurl" because of the nausea it could cause. (Zagorsky.)

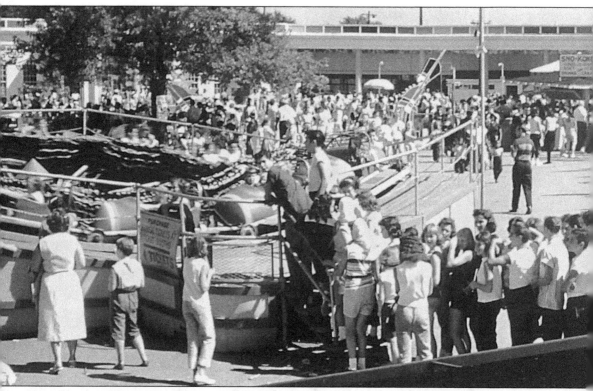

The first Caterpillar ride arrived in 1923. A newer version arrived in 1948 and remained until the park's closure. Hyla F. Maynes of New York invented the ride in 1925. It consisted of 18 separate, capsule-like cars arranged on a circular track. Each car was attached to a metal arm that extended inward to a central location, much like the axle on a spoked bicycle wheel. A round metal collapsible fan-type "pinwheel" device was mounted to the rear of each car. The collapsible pinwheel was operated by a series of wire ropes that, as the caterpillar rolled along its wavy track, caused an attached cover to slowly unfold and enclose the riders, giving the ride the appearance of a caterpillar. Centrifugal force would cause riders to slide outward, squeezing against each other. An occasional blast of air from a fan mounted under the ride would surprise riders. Prior to the end of the ride, the canopy would retract. Only two working Caterpillar rides are known to exist. (Menning.)

The adult-sized whip arrived in 1919 and was replaced by newer versions over the years. This photograph from 1962 shows riders bracing for the coming whip action from leaving the curve. There were 12 open-top carriages, each with a long, flat, metal spring-action bar protruding from under the front of the carriage. A metal safety grab bar helped to secure the riders. (Toth.)

In 1978, the Flying Scooter ride was placed at the northeast end of the park, near Hooterville Highway. Idora dubbed the ride the Fantastic Flying Machines. Eight metal gondolas were suspended in the air from cables attached to a center post with metal arms. Each gondola had one front moveable "fin" and one fixed rear fin. The gondolas swung through the sky in a circle. (Zagorsky.)

The Skydiver was a Ferris wheel type ride with enclosed rider compartments. A steering wheel inside allowed the rider to spin the compartment if desired. The Skydiver survived one season, arriving in 1968 and sold off before opening day in 1969. During its short stay, the Skydiver saw limited ridership and lots of cleanups due to ill riders. It was not a popular ride. (Schwartz.)

The Orbit was new to the park in 1960, but it only lasted two seasons for its first visit. It returned by 1964, but after that, confusion reigns. The ride supposedly left after another season or two but is seen again in photographs from the 1970s. The mystery continues. (Zagorsky.)

Lee Eyerly's aircraft company built training devices for pilots. He was approached in the early 1930s about selling some of his unique designs as amusement rides. After his first successful sale, he switched his business model and gave up the aircraft business. The Rock-O-Plane was a 1947 invention. Idora Park's ride arrived in 1976 and sold for $16,000 at auction. (Nard.)

The Spider was a ride made by Eyerly Aircraft Company. It arrived at the park in 1974. It had six outstretched steel arms with two passenger compartments attached to the end of each arm. The ride sold for $61,000 at Idora Park's auction, more than double that of any other ride, and second only to the carousel. (Hardy.)

The Rocket Ship was a variation of the Circle Swing invented by Harry Traver in 1902. The first Circle Swing came to Idora between 1903 and 1910 in the southwest part of the park, near the Ingersol coaster. It had a tall center mast with outstretched arms at the top from which metal cables hung down and attached to wicker gondola baskets. The baskets carried riders in a circle. The next variation of the ride was built on the upper midway near the Funhouse. It was replaced with three futuristic looking rocket ships made by the R.E. Chambers Company in Beaver Falls, Pennsylvania. (Above, Olson; below, Menning.)

A larger and sturdier 85-foot tower was built for the heavy rocket ships. Each rocket was suspended to a height of about 20 feet above the ground and inches above a landing pad that served as a roof for the concession stands below. A flat circular roof was in place approximately 25 feet above the landing pad. The roof kept the cables away from the tower and in the correct "launch" and "land" positions. When launching or landing, the suspended cables made a distinctive rubbing noise against the edge of the circular structure, a sound that no rider could ever forget. Each rocket had four seats that could carry two or three passengers. A small triangular loading door was the only restraint. (Above, Dyce; below, Hardy.)

The year 1967 was the first year for the Paratrooper ride at Idora, which remained until the park's closure in 1984. The ride was manufactured by the Frank Hrubetz Company in Oregon. There were 10 suspended canopies with seating for two people in each seat. The ride was located on the upper midway alongside the large white building that served as a ladies' restroom (at left above). Kiddieland was close by, as seen by the distinctive roofline of the picnic building at right. The Paratrooper gave the rider a sense of flying when rising, and of floating when descending. The ride sold for $8,500 at auction. (Above, Nard; below, Dyce.)

The Scrambler (above) was invented in 1938 but was not sold on the market until 1954. Idora Park's Scrambler arrived in 1971 and was placed in front of the newly renovated Helter Skelter bumper car building. The Scrambler had 12 cars separated into three groups of four. The cars were suspended from one horizontal arm each. The ride spun the cars in circles toward each other. The Ferris wheel was a simple but favorite ride among grownups and children alike. The 1958 photograph below reveals that L-shaped hair guards were not yet in place on the top of the seat sides and back. That would change after several riders were injured when their long hair was caught in the exposed couplings. (Above, Maffitt; below, Menning.)

Idora Park had one of the very first water rides in the country when the Panama Canal ride was built in 1915. The water ride was re-themed with scenes from *The Wizard of Oz* in 1923. In 1930, the Rapids water ride was built, replacing the Wizard of Oz on roughly the same site. The Rapids features included dark winding tunnels, unexpected props, sound effects, and a splashdown drop in front of a large windmill with a colorfully lighted, cascading waterfall. The Rapids immediately became a favorite for many park patrons who eagerly lined up for the ride. (Left, Goddard; below, TIPE.)

Some of the largest crowds arrived on company picnic days, and as usual, the boat ride was a huge draw at this 1974 Copperweld Steel company picnic. The Rapids became the Lost River in 1968, still a water ride, but with a jungle theme. The boats had not changed much since they were built in 1930, and the waterfall was still in place. The windmill was converted to a grass hut with an animatronic jungle native in front, playing drums. There was also a huge animatronic elephant on top of the pillared façade, entirely hidden from view here, unfortunately. (Both, Maffitt.)

SCENIC COASTER, IDORA PARK, YOUNGSTOWN, OHIO.

This rare postcard describes the image as the "Scenic Coaster." It was actually named the Dip-the-Dips, and the reason for that name is obvious by the hills and drops shown here. The Dip-the-Dips was a side-friction, magnetic-braking roller coaster with a 4,000-foot track made of pine and built entirely with nuts, bolts, and washers by the T.M. Harton Company. No nails were used in the construction. The ride had two three-car trains that ran about 23 miles per hour. The Dip-the-Dips opened to the public in 1914 and was reconstructed 10 years later, in 1924, to become the Jack Rabbit roller coaster. The coaster was referred to as the "Dips-of-Death" after the 1915 collision between two trains that caused the death of one young man and seriously injured 16 riders. (TIPE.)

The above 1927 photograph of the Firefly Figure-Eight roller coaster façade (left) presents an ironic glimpse of where that façade would be in three years' time, in 1930—at the front of the loading station for the Wildcat roller coaster, which replaced the Firefly. Lillian Desmond's name appears on the side of the theater building at right as testament to her status as the park's most popular actress. Below, the wood-tiered structure of the Firefly (left) is shown from a point farther south on the midway. The ballroom (right) was built in 1910. In another ironic twist, the Rapids and Wildcat, which were built on the site of the dismantled Firefly, were destroyed on that site in 1984—by fire. (Both, Mulichak.)

The Jack Rabbit was Idora Park's fourth roller coaster to be built. The Three-Way Figure-Eight Toboggan Slide was built in 1902 and was replaced by the Firefly Figure-Eight coaster in 1920. The T.M. Harton Company built the Dip-the-Dips coaster for 1914. The Jack Rabbit was really a $75,000 reconfiguration of the old Dip-the-Dips coaster, rebuilt in 1924. The "new" Jack Rabbit was 90 feet high with a 70-foot drop. Each of Idora Park's large coasters recorded a death. The Jack Rabbit was no exception. Sixteen-year-old Richard Nelson was killed in July 1963 when he was thrown from his seat after allegedly standing up on the curves, facing the wrong direction. The Dip-the-Dips had one death in 1915 when the lead coaster failed to climb a hill and rolled back into another coaster that was descending toward it. The Firefly's manager was struck by two coasters and killed while inspecting the track in 1920. (Sakowski.)

By 1929, Rex Billings, Idora Park's manager and part owner, felt it was time to add a new, first-class roller coaster. A delay in the Wildcat's construction (and the Rapids water ride) was caused when the Firefly coaster site was not immediately available. Herbert Schmeck of the Philadelphia Toboggan Company designed the new coaster and work began in 1930. The Wildcat was designated PTC Coaster No. 83 and became an immediate favorite of park-goers with its 95-foot height and 55-mile-per-hour top speed. In 1940, the Wildcat was altered to remove the frightening first drop, a banking curve, which was replaced with a more angled descent. Tragedy struck the coaster in 1948 when 20-year-old Royal Dinkelman was thrown from his seat after allegedly placing his knees over the restraining bar and standing up. The Wildcat had only one stationary restraint bar for each row of seats. There were no seatbelts or other safety devices. The death was ruled an accident. (Sakowski.)

The carousel pavilion, seen at right above, was built in 1910 and housed two separate carousels during its existence. In the background (center) is a glimpse of the theater. The building at left was built in 1921 as a cafeteria, located next to the Photo Gallery. From 1933 through 1984, it was the Penny Arcade. For many years, the Fool the Guesser and Guess Your Weight station was located in the spot just in front of the two boxes mounted on the arcade's outer wall. When the "Guesser" was working, the boxes were opened wide to show the prizes inside as a way to entice patrons. (Above, Jenkins; below, Nard.)

Very few photographs have been found that were taken inside the poorly lighted Penny Arcade, built in 1921. These photographs are from 1983. The entertainment inside cost anywhere from one penny on the antique machines to a quarter for the modern games. Nickel and dime machines were also in abundance. Cash was the currency, as tokens were not used in the Penny Arcade. Automatic change machines were never used; patrons could change their dollars and quarters at the always-attended cashier's cage for the many shooting and bombing games, claw machines, roto-merchandisers, grip strength testers, sports machines, card dispensers, and so much more. On October 20, 1984, more than 70 arcade items, including all machines and the cashier's cage, were sold at auction. (Both, Zagorsky.)

The Funhouse was built by the Philadelphia Toboggan Company in 1922 at a cost of $23,329.39. Located on the northwest corner of the upper midway at the spot where the Pony Track had once been, the attraction was officially named All For Fun by park management. Park-goers unofficially renamed it "the Funhouse," and the name stuck. Roller-skating had become a national craze, and in order to keep up, the Funhouse was converted to a roller-skating rink in 1931. In 1938, the Funhouse regained the building and was remodeled. Many more changes would come to the Funhouse in the coming years, including a Laffin' Sal animatronic figure that the park renamed "Laffin' Lena," a matronly looking woman who bent slightly forward at the waist and laughed continuously. Laffin' Lena disappeared from public view in 1968 but reappeared many years later for a short time prior to the park's closure. In this 1950 photograph, she can be seen as she was normally displayed, in an elevated glass enclosure. (Eiler.)

This August 1958 photograph shows the exterior of the Funhouse as it appeared through most of the 1960s. Laffin' Lena can be seen above the entrance, in the enclosure between the words "Fun" and "House." The Tunnel of Love ride is on the right, at the end of the Funhouse building. To the right of the Tunnel of Love is a portion of the Basketball Throw game. The first-aid station is the white building at far left. The right half of the original Funhouse had its final remodel as Laffin' Lena's Loonyland. (Above, Menning; below Nard.)

The right half of the Funhouse became the Whacky Shack in 1968. It was constructed by Bill Tracey of Outdoor Dimensions, who re-themed the Rapids into the Lost River that same year. The Whacky Shack was a walkthrough attraction with a mirror maze, strobe lights, and other modern gags. The left half of the Funhouse was re-themed five years earlier by Tracey as the Gold Nugget, a dark ride that is partly visible here. In 1972, the Gold Nugget became the Kooky Castle with a new façade and new gags, including skeletons and a large fake bat that dropped from the ceiling when a floor switch was triggered. The Kooky Castle remained until the park closed in 1984. (Above, MVHS; below, Dyce.)

The Cheyenne Shootout was an electronic rifle gallery that took up residence in 1974 on the east side of the lower midway, where the Turbo ride had operated the previous few years. Shooters used a realistic-looking rifle to aim at whichever of the tiny targets they chose. When the target was hit, it triggered a noise, light, or movement from the nearest animatronic figure. Several targets caused varmints to collapse, and one made the piano player start playing. The park was more cautious about live ammunition after the 1920 shooting death of an employee. The 1958 photograph below shows the booth operator patiently awaiting customers at the park's pellet-gun target range. (Above, Nard; below, Menning.)

The view above of the lower midway facing north shows movie posters for H.G. Wells's *The Invisible Man* on the theater wall in 1933 (right). Sam Warner of Warner Bros. operated the projector in this theater before moving on to Hollywood fame. America was just a few years into the Great Depression, yet crowds were still quite large. The 1927 photograph below shows roughly the same area from a position farther north. The roof of the carousel pavilion can be seen in the background at left with a man sitting on the bench next to it. The building in the background (center) is the cafeteria, and behind it is a sign for the Whip ride. The Ferris wheel is in the background at right. (Above, Jenkins; below, Mulichak.)

This 1939 view of the crowded lower midway is facing south. Most park-goers were still dressing up for the special day out. The Wildcat roller coaster is on the right. The carousel pavilion in the background (left of center) completely obscures the park's second most popular ride, the Rapids. The roof overhang at far left is the Penny Arcade. (Jenkins.)

This 1933 view of the lower midway is facing south. The 10 Skee-Ball games that arrived five years earlier in 1926 were located in the building to the immediate left of the castellated rooftop façade (right). Behind Skee-Ball was the splashdown hill of the Rapids water ride. Author Jim Amey worked at this Skee-Ball booth in the summer of 1976. (Jenkins.)

At least one uniformed police officer was always present during opening hours. The officer above patrols north along the lower midway past a row of games in 1958. The photograph below from the Copperweld Steel company picnic in 1973 shows a northern view of the lower midway. The Lost River's roof-covered hill and the Wildcat's south turn are visible behind the park office (left). The Turbo ride (right) was moved farther south for the following season, and the Cheyenne Shootout was built on that site in 1974. Next to the Turbo is the Sno-Kones concession stand. (Above, Menning; below, Maffitt.)

The little boy at far right above appears to be eyeing the coin-operated rides in this 1958 photograph. At the end of the day, it was the employees' task to gather up the empty pop bottle cases, like those sitting under the "souvenirs" sign. The top of the Rocket Ship tower (left), located on the upper midway, can be seen above the row of game booths. Below, another 1958 view of the lower midway, facing south, shows (clockwise) the Sno-Kones concession, the Tilt-A-Whirl ride, the ballroom building, Play Golf and a ticket booth, the Rapids façade, the park office, and Sportland. (Both, Menning.)

Author Jim Amey worked Skee-Ball Alley in the summer of 1976 after being fired from the Football Throw game for winning prizes while off-duty. Nine wooden balls for 10¢ could produce a winner if a player scored 180 points. Tickets were awarded based on the player's score, and those tickets were then turned in for prizes. A score of 450 was a perfect game. After a summer of constant

practice, Amey rolled eight balls, hitting the maximum points of 50 on each. With one ball left to roll he choked, scoring a 40 and ruining what would have been a perfect score. Not realizing it until two decades later, the summer of 1976 sowed the seeds of passion for what would become his mission to save whatever remained of Idora Park. (Menning.)

The sign on the wall inside the midway game booth above reads, "Win a Big One—Every Win Can Take Choice." Plenty of teddy bears were available at this booth, and these two young ladies seem to be interested in something, but it is unclear what the game might be. Also unclear is why the child at center is walking around wearing a teddy bear head and hands. The young woman on the right below appears very happy with her new teddy bear. (Both, Menning.)

The Fish Pond was one of the most popular games at the park. The fishing pole consisted of a short wooden stick with a foot-long length of string attached. A small hook was at the end of the string. The fish were two inches long with a hook in their mouth. Some fish were glass, and some were plastic. All had numbers that coincided with prizes on the shelves. Catching fish No. 25 won the choice of prize. Below, Pat Licek's fish (left) and Rick Grooms's fish (right) were donated to The Idora Park Experience by their owners. A third fish was donated by Kay Mumaw but was on vacation during this photo shoot. (Above, Menning; below, TIPE.)

Over 12 Wins was a lower midway game. The object of the game was to roll three rubber balls, normally one at a time, down a wooden playfield with 13 holes at the opposite end. A vertical panel at the end of the board had a series of numbered lights. When the ball dropped into a hole, an electric contact would close and send a signal to the corresponding light. Prizes were determined by the sum of the lighted numbers (above). The vertical panel changed over the years, but the object of the game remained the same. Bill Prest donated the Idora Park original Over 12 Wins playfield seen below to The Idora Park Experience. (Above, Menning; below, TIPE.)

Spill The Milk was a difficult game to win. Some establishments illegally weighted the milk bottles so that winning was impossible, but Idora Park never did such a thing. Five metal "milk" bottles were placed on a flat surface in a vertical pyramid pattern with three bottles on the bottom and two on top. The player had three opportunities to knock all five milk bottles from the flat surface in order to win a prize. Simply knocking them down was not enough to win; the bottles had to be on the ground. Winning at the Toss The Rings game (below) involved tossing small wooden rings with just the right arc to get at least one to land over the neck of a pop bottle and stay there. (Both, Menning.)

The Wildcat, the Jack Rabbit, the Rapids/Lost River, the Rocket Ships, the Ballroom, and the French fries are the subjects most people reminisce about when remembering Idora Park, and not necessarily in that order. The French fry stand in the 1970s served fries that customers soaked in vinegar, something new to most people. The fries came in a paper cone that the attendant placed in one of a line of three long boards just outside the serving window. The boards had holes drilled through for the paper cone to rest in. When asked about the secret recipe that lets no other fries compare, one former owner of the park revealed that the cheapest ingredients were used and the grease was not changed for the entire season. The recipe can be found in *Recipes of Youngstown* Volume I, on page 273. The French fry stand is seen below in its final days, in 1984. (Above, Dyce; below, Nard.)

The dance pavilion was the park's oldest building, constructed in 1899. It was moved to the northwest corner of the park, where a suspicious fire in 1986 destroyed it as it sat abandoned after the park's closure. Between 1899 and 1984, the building served as a dance pavilion, the casino theater, a roller-skating rink, and a restaurant. It became the German-themed Heidelberg Gardens in 1933 after Prohibition ended. Beer was served at the Heidelberg, and it became the largest eatery in the park. During World War II, with America at war, management felt that the German name might be offensive to some patriotic patrons, and it was changed to Idora Gardens. The name Heidelberg Gardens returned four years after the war, in 1949. The establishment's name would change one final time, in 1981, when it became the Crazy Horse Saloon. (Menning.)

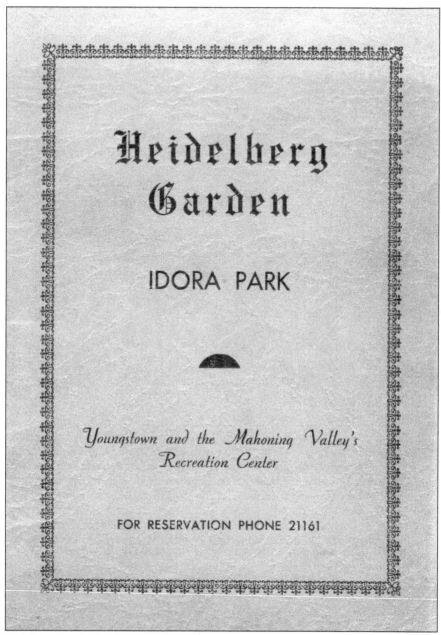

Heidelberg Garden

IDORA PARK

Youngstown and the Mahoning Valley's Recreation Center

FOR RESERVATION PHONE 21161

This Heidelberg Garden booklet from 1934 lists many advertisers from the Youngstown area. As was the practice of the day, all of the companies had five-digit phone numbers. Most of the businesses closed since this booklet was published, but a few remain. Some of the more interesting ads for Youngstown include Lewis Hair Tinting Parlors on North Phelps Street, Youngstown Typesetting on Market Street, Renner's Youngstown Lager Beer, and Allmakes Typewriter & Adding Machines Company on West Commerce Street. Only two businesses seem to have survived since 1934: Emch Brothers Spring Works and Schwebel's Bakery. Emch Brothers are at the same location on West Myrtle Avenue, and its phone number has the same last four digits. A few of the scheduled picnics listed include Catholic Day, South Side Day, Women's Driving Exhibition, Slovak Day, Colored Day, Russian Day, Irish Day, and Polish Day. (TIPE.)

STARTING
SUNDAY, MAY 17th 1964
THE

FREE ADMISSION

"KOVE"

FREE ADMISSION

Goes South For The Summer !
MAKE IT TO
THE KOVE SOUTH
LOCATED IN THE HEIDELBERG GARDENS, IDORA PARK
COLLEGIATE ENTERTAINMENT BY
MIKE RONCONE and his ORCHESTRA
9:30 UNTIL ? - CASUAL DRESS PERMITTED

In 1964, Idora felt the need to open a second dance location for the 20s-and-under crowd, so the Heidelberg Gardens began hosting the Kove South for the growing popularity of rock-n-roll music. Local legend Mike Roncone and his orchestra provided live music one night a week. The music was advertised with a 9:30 p.m. start and had no designated time to stop. Phil Keaggy also performed at the Kove South, as did the Human Beingz. In 1981, the Heidelberg Gardens underwent its final transition when it took on an old west theme complete with an old chuck wagon, skeleton, and broken-down horse at a poisoned waterhole. The name was changed to the Crazy Horse Saloon. (Above, Roncone; below, Zagorsky.)

Above, kids and adults flock to this stand for a free sample of B.A. Milliken's ice cream in the 1920s, handed out by uniformed employees of the Youngstown Sanitary Milk Company. The swimming pool building is barely visible in the background. Below, taking a break from the excitement of a day at Idora Park on May 20, 1951, Ross (left) and Ed enjoy a beer outside the Heidelberg Gardens restaurant. The sign for the bingo game, "Play Idora," can be seen at upper left. Maybe this was a break while their wives played Idora? (Above, Jenkins; below, Eiler.)

Idora's owners wisely included concession stands around the base of the ride when the tower structure that would become the Rocket Ship was built. Unfortunately, customers at these concessions had to be wary of any knucklehead riding above who thought it was funny to spit or spill something on those walking below. Anyone caught doing so was removed from the park. Betty Pape operated the Coffee and Do-Nut stand, shown here in 1956 with her crew. There never seemed to be a shortage of teenagers ready to work in any of the park's jobs, whether it was concessions, games, rides, maintenance, or customer service. (Both, Parks.)

The concessions under the Rocket Ship were known as the Lunching Pad, combining the rocket loading (or launching) area with food. Most people did not notice the spelling and get the joke, or just did not care. This stand sold Pennsylvania Dutch funnel cakes, coffee, sloppy joe sandwiches, hamburgers, pizza, draft beer, and soft drinks. Inside the same stand below and facing the camera is Mickey Rindin, son of Idora Park part-owner Max Rindin. The Rindin family was in charge of all concessions at the park, except for a few that were privately owned. (Both, Zagorsky.)

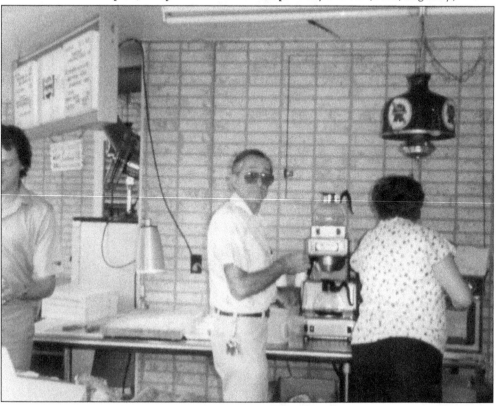

Notice how the apples in these two photographs have been dipped all the way up to the stick so that the entire apple is covered. This is important. The first opening of The Idora Park Experience was April 26, 2014, the 30th anniversary of the fire that caused Idora Park to close. Author Jim Amey found a supplier for candy apples to be sold at the museum's opening but noticed that the apples were not dipped like Idora's, all the way to the stick like the one Robin is eating below. The supplier's apples were rejected until they had been re-dipped properly, just like Idora's. (Above, Dyce; below, Zagorsky.)

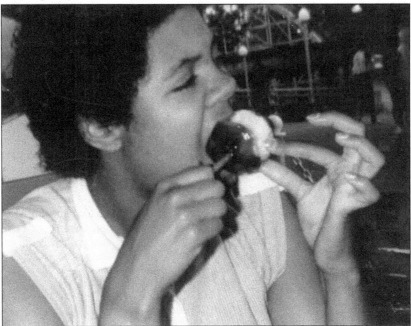

The popcorn stand was on the east side of the lower midway next to the Shoot The Star shooting game. No one ever won anything at Shoot The Star because no matter how good a player was, the booth attendant always managed to find a tiny piece of red star still remaining on the target. The best part about the game was getting to fire a machine gun, even though it only fired BBs. The popcorn booth, shown here in 1958, had the coolest-looking neon sign when it was lighted at night. Besides popcorn, it sold candy apples, caramel corn, and peanuts for 15¢ per serving in 1958. Idora Park popcorn boxes are rare and have become very collectible. (Above, Menning; left TIPE.)

Doris Turney brought cotton candy to Idora Park in 1929 and sold it from a stand near the ballroom. She called the sweet, sticky confection candy floss, but eventually, the name changed to cotton candy. Her stand was run over by a beer truck so she moved to the upper midway under the Rocket Ships, where she would remain until the park closed in 1984. Turney retired before Idora closed, leaving the business to her grandson and great-granddaughter Tammi Anderson. The latter has retained the original cotton candy equipment and recipe and sells her product at special events under her business name, Little Idora. She also sells her cotton candy at The Idora Park Experience museum. (Both, Anderson.)

The picnic grounds were situated on a hill that ran parallel to and east of the lower midway. Rumor has it that the hill was an ancient Indian burial ground for a tribe called the Idora Indians, but no one knows for sure that there ever was such a tribe, and there has been no excavation of the site to prove or disprove the rumor. These stone steps led up to the picnic grounds. Going down these steps led to the ballroom, just a few yards straight ahead, and turning a sharp left led to the Jack Rabbit roller coaster. The covered pavilions seen below sat at the top of the picnic hill. (Above, Dyce; below, TIPE.)

The picnic areas were filled with park-goers for every company picnic. This Copperweld Steel company picnic from the 1970s shows a few families enjoying the weather and each other's company under some shade trees. The Wildcat roller coaster can be seen in the background above. The roof of the Arcade building is visible between the Wildcat and the picnic tables. People sitting on the ground at left are waiting for the train to roll by. The tracks were on the side of the hill directly in front of where they are sitting. The three large covered picnic pavilions filled up quickly on company picnic days. Seating under the shaded area was on a first come, first served basis. (Both, Maffitt.)

Idora 1984 Family Discount Coupon

Good Sat, July 28
Save $3.95 per person during the
WEAN UNITED
Annual Family Picnic
FREE Beer, Orange-ade or Coffee 1 to 5pm

ENJOY ALL RIDES
FROM 1 TO 10PM FOR

3.00 person
or free admission
REGULARLY $6.95

Kids under 4 ride FREE / Rt. 62, Youngstown, OH

Please present ticket at gate

Employee Family Day

IDORA PARK
SEPT. 8, 1984
1:00pm-10:00pm

name _____
dept. _____

St. Elizabeth Hospital
Medical Center

Since Idora Park's beginning, its owners used every marketing method available to bring in patrons and increase revenue. Company picnics brought the largest crowds, but those crowds were waning with the numerous steel mill closures of the late 1970s and the loss of businesses affected by those closures. To drum up business, potential visitors were offered discount coupons to company picnics, such as the Wean United picnic in 1984. The final picnic for Idora Park was for employees of St. Elizabeth Hospital and their families on September 8, 1984. This was also the last day that the park operated. (Above, Doll; left, TIPE.)

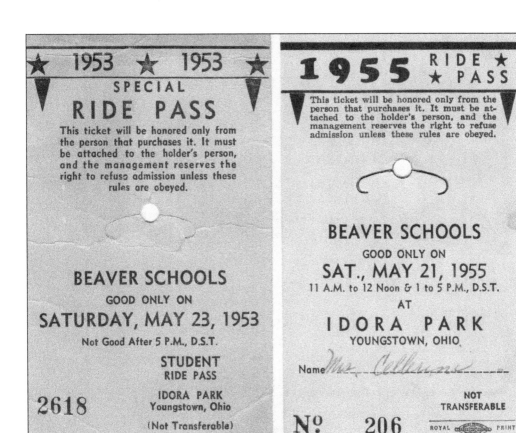

Nearly every possible ethnic group and elementary school had a special day reserved at the park, and they all received discounted tickets of some type. Idora did what it could to pull in kids from nearby Pennsylvania, too. Cascade Park in New Castle had been a direct competitor with Idora since both parks' earliest days. They were rivals from the start and fewer than 30 miles apart. In 1953 and 1955, Beaver, Pennsylvania, schools received ride passes. Parochial Schools Day was reserved for religious schools. Teachers and responsible adult chaperones were admitted free. (Above, TIPE; right, Carnahan)

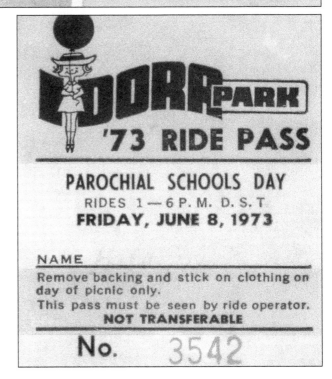

Partnering with local companies to offer discounts was a way for Idora and the participating businesses to increase patronage and revenue. Participating establishments offered Idora Park admission, ride, or concession discounts in exchange for purchasing a product or service. Amoco service stations were one of the most favored partners. Fill up with gasoline on your way to Idora! Burger Chef restaurants offered a $1.45 discount on an all-day ride pass at Idora with the purchase of a large drink. And who buys a large drink without also buying a burger and fries? (Both, MVHS.)

BUDGET POLISH
Penn-Ohio POLKA FESTIVAL
Sunday, July 17th, 1983
12 continuous hours: noon to midnight

NOON to 12:45 — TOM BALICKY & HARMONY TONES	— 6:00 to 6:45
12:45 to 1:30 — THE CLEVELAND SOUND	— 6:45 to 7:30
1:30 to 2:15 — ANDY and THE TRELTONES	— 7:30 to 8:15
2:15 to 3:00 — HENRY and THE VERSA J's	— 8:15 to 9:00
3:00 to 3:45 — BUD HUNDENSKI . . . featuring MATT WASIELEWSKI	— 9:00 to 9:45
3:45 to 4:30 — THE JOLLY J's	— 9:45 to 10:30
4:30 to 5:15 — THE POLISH FRIENDS	— 10:30 to 11:15
5:15 to 6:00 — THE RAYTONES	— 11:15 to MIDNIGHT

(Note: Schedule is approximate and subject to change. Joe Oberaitis previously scheduled will not appear due to his disbandment and relocation.)

Adults pay one price... $3.95*

*(Advance Tickets $3.50 from participating bands.)

Price includes admission to both Park and Ballroom for entire day. Children under 12 admitted free when accompanied by parents.

One of the Best Dance Floors in the Penn-Ohio Area

IDORA ballroom
rt. 62, youngstown's south side

The ballroom had hosted just about every kind of music imaginable by the 1980s. There were big band orchestras, jazz musicians, country, disco, pop, and rock, and then there was polka music. Polka was so popular that it even had its own festivals, starting in 1967 with Larry Walk, namesake of *Larry Walk's Happy Polkaland* radio program. The first-ever event was a 12-hour nonstop Polka-thon. Polka music and dancing were so popular that the park even took out billboard advertising for the festivals. These festivals ran every summer until the park closed. (Above, TIPE; below, MVHS.)

This 1925 partial blueprint of the theater that was built in 1899 and renovated several times shows how large it was, with a seating capacity of 1,007. The theater was on the east side of the lower midway, extending up into the hillside behind it, and across from where the Rapids/ Lost River ride would be built five years later. The theater's concrete supports are still in place today. The *Youngstown Daily Vindicator* ran an advertisement for a Ku Klux Klan picnic to be held on August 8, 1924, at Idora Park. The ad states, "Everybody Welcome." Somehow, that seems more than a little unlikely. (Left, Eynon; below, TIPE.)

Klan Picnic
IDORA PARK
AUGUST 8, 1924

Everybody Welcome--Lots of Good Music
Special Sports and Col. C. A. Gunder
Will Speak---Other Good Speakers
Come Everybody!
Enjoy All Day At Idora Park

Serious sporting events (and not-so-serious sporting events) took place at Idora. Baseball and football games were regular attractions, and on occasion, wrestling too. Special boxing events included John L. Sullivan, the former bare-knuckle boxing champion who boxed an exhibition in 1906. Jim Corbett, another heavyweight boxing champion, visited the park in 1929. In 1947, middleweight boxing champ Rocky Graziano boxed an exhibition. Youngstown's mayor tried to ban boxing in 1922 after a poorly fought match was held at Idora, but the ban did not last long, and the fights soon resumed. On September 9, 1936, the park advertised 42 rounds of boxing for a ticket price of $1. On a somewhat comedic note, the California Cuties, a team of men dressed as women playing softball, entertained crowds in 1982. (Above, TIPE; right, MVHS.)

WORLD'S FUNNIEST SOFTBALL TEAM

CALIFORNIA CUTIES NOVELTY SOFTBALL TEAM

"Those Who Watch the Cuties Play, Live to Laugh Another Day"

CALIFORNIA CUTIES ARE THE ORIGINAL MEN'S NOVELTY SOFTBALL TEAM PLAYING IN LADIES' CLOTHES

FOUR MAN TEAM — FOUR MAN TEAM

CALIFORNIA CUTIES

vs. WHOT / WSRD
Date FRIDAY, JULY 9th
Place IDORA PARK
Time 6:30   Admission: Adults 3.50   Children 2.50

CALIFORNIA CUTIES, P.O. BOX 455, LAKEWOOD, CALIFORNIA 90714

THE IDORA AMUSEMENT CO.
IDORA PARK
YOUNGSTOWN, OHIO

15909

The Dollar Savings and Trust Company
Youngstown, Ohio

May 23 19 77   56-47
                 412

PAY_____ IDORA 5000 AND 00 CTS _____ DOLLARS $ 5,000.00

TO THE ORDER OF
Dynamic Displays
2725 W. Fort St.
Detroit, Mich. 48216

THE IDORA AMUSEMENT CO.
TREASURER

NOT NEGOTIABLE

⑆0412⑈0047⑆ 010 020 060⑈

THE IDORA AMUSEMENT CO.
YOUNGSTOWN, OHIO

| INVOICE | | DESCRIPTION | TOTAL AMOUNT | DEDUCTIONS | | NET AMOUNT |
DATE	NO.			DISCOUNT	FREIGHT	
5-23		Final payment for Space Shuttle building				

Not all decisions at the park worked out; for example, the Klan picnic in 1924 or letting children ride on the back of a bear in the earliest years. On May 23, 1977, Idora's owners wrote a $5,000 check to Dynamic Displays as final payment for a space shuttle building. On the same date, a check for $15,000 was written as partial payment to the same company for the building. For some unknown reason, the $5,000 payment was voided immediately, and the attraction never materialized. Occasionally, plans for a new ride or attraction could fall through. In 1916, for example, the park wanted to eliminate the Dip-the-Dips coaster, and announced a replacement coaster that never came about: the Race Through the Clouds. (Above, TIPE; below, MVHS.)

To

Orville

Karla Wallenda

Besides having theater, pony rides, dancing, a zoo, billiards, a bowling alley, rides, games, and concessions, Idora booked several death-defying acts—anything to bring in more patronage for the park. One act involved a female balloonist who parachuted from her balloon, cut the parachute away, and went into a free fall before deploying a second chute and landing safely. Another act was the 50-foot high dive into a tank with four feet of water. There were even diving horses and a diving elk. Karla (also spelled Carla) Wallenda of the Flying Wallenda family has been a daredevil since she was three years old, and is still performing in her 80s without a net or safety harness. In 2017, at age 81, she performed a headstand and other stunts from atop an 85-foot-pole, again with no safety devices. After her pole climbing performance at the Idora Park ball field in the 1950s, she autographed this promotional photograph for fan Orville Ritchie. (Ritchie.)

WHOT DAY
Wednesday, August 19th, 1970
IDORA PARK
Starring
BOBBY SHERMAN
ADVANCE ADMISSION $3.50 PERSON
This Ticket Good For Idora Rides - 1 to 11 p.m.
And Admission to **3:00 p.m.** Bobby Sherman Show
—— Retain This Portion of Ticket —— 10

No. 640

WHOT was a popular Youngstown area radio station in the 1950s, 1960s, and 1970s, at 1330 on the AM dial. They played pop and rock music and hosted record hops at the ballroom as early as the mid-1950s. Idora held WHOT Day events at the park, where local music bands and nationally known acts alike would perform their songs. During WHOT Day in August 1970, teenage heartthrob, actor, and singer Bobby Sherman drew huge crowds for two concerts. In August 1971, another teen heartthrob, actor-turned-singer David Cassidy performed in concert. (Both, Carnahan.)

WHOT DAY
Sunday, August 29th, 1971
IDORA PARK
Starring
David Cassidy
ADVANCE ADMISSION $5.00 PERSON
This Ticket Good For All Idora Rides - 1 to 11 p.m.
And Admission to **2:00 p.m.** David Cassidy Show
— Retain This Portion of Ticket — 10

A - 3248

WHOT's . . . .

SPRING THING

SATURDAY, APRIL 29th, 1972

This Ticket Good For All Rides - 1 to 6 p.m.

ADVANCE ADM. $2.50   AT GATE $3.00

- Retain This Portion of Ticket -

No. 1132

Boots Bell was arguably the most popular Youngstown area disk jockey from the 1960s and onward. His signature lines "Yes indeedy doody daddy," "Have yourself a happy," and "You've just had your bell rung," distinguished him from other disk jockeys and endeared him to many listeners. His huge following made him the obvious choice to host many of the annual WHOT Spring Thing concerts early each year, as well as the annual WHOT Day concerts later in the summer. A handful of those event performers—like the Eagles, who played in 1972—went on to international success. (Both, Carnahan.)

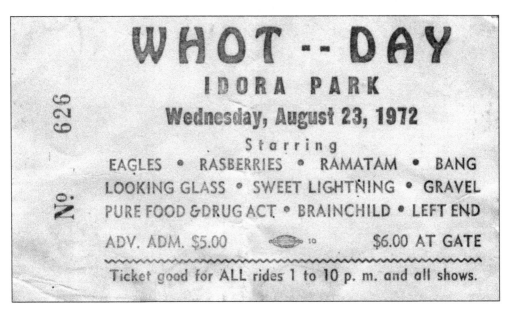

WHOT -- DAY

IDORA PARK

Wednesday, August 23, 1972

Starring

EAGLES • RASBERRIES • RAMATAM • BANG
LOOKING GLASS • SWEET LIGHTNING • GRAVEL
PURE FOOD & DRUG ACT • BRAINCHILD • LEFT END

ADV. ADM. $5.00 $6.00 AT GATE

Ticket good for ALL rides 1 to 10 p. m. and all shows.

No. 626

This 1909 calendar shows the Charles D. Hoover children. It was donated by Charles's great-granddaughter Carol Morris. Many employees and their families lived in temporary shacks, or "tent cottages," in Idora Park during spring and summer. Transient employees and theater performers would come and go, leaving their own particular artwork on the buildings. The Hoover family operated the photography gallery for more than four decades. The young boy at center in the back row is six-year-old John Hoover. The taller boy is his older brother Paul. Both eventually found work at Idora Park. In 1920, at age 18, John was shot while working at the .22-rifle shooting gallery. The shooter was never identified. Authorities speculated that the shooting was an accident and that the shooter panicked and fled. John was taken to the photograph gallery to be seen by his parents and then transported to the hospital by his brother, where he died from his injuries. (Morris.)

As Idora Park's popularity grew by leaps and bounds from 1899 onwards, the need for varied forms of entertainment at the casino theater, dance hall, and ballroom increased. Musicians and actors contracted for specific periods of time, sometimes for an entire season. These transient acts needed lodging, as did contractors from out of town who built the rides and attractions. This souvenir postcard is typical of many that the park's Hoover Photo Gallery produced in the early 1900s for those who lived on the property. It was taken on Pearce Road, a plot of land that was purchased during one of the park's expansions. In it, a family is lounging on the ground as they watch acrobats practice their routine. Meanwhile, a young man sitting in a tree at left looks up from his newspaper at the photographer. Many residents left their "calling card" on the exterior walls of their dwelling, as seen at right. (Morris.)

6. Operators of rides catering to small children must be especially attentive. These operators should assist the child in getting on and off the rides.

7. Smell of Smoke - Fire is our worst enemy. If at any time you should smell smoke...check into it immediately. You should be familiar with all fire extinguisher locations, the operation and the use of all fire extinguishers. If you don't know....ask now!

8. The operator and ticket takers should pay special attention to the following type persons:
   a) Pregnant women
   b) People with limbs in cast or braces
   c) Persons showing the slightest signs of drunkeness
   These above people should NOT be allowed to ride if the operator or ticket taker thinks that the type of ride they are going to board is too much for them.

9. No food or beverages allowed on the rides by patrons.

10. Operation of a ride is a position of extreme responsibility. There is to be NO visiting with guests or friends while it is in operation. No unauthorized personnel are to be within the confines of the ride. Violation of this rule is grounds for termination or suspension.

4

DON'T OVERLOAD YOUR RIDE

USE SAFETY BELTS AND BARS

5

The employee handbook used cartoon illustrations to help instruct employees in the rules of the park. Safety is listed as the number-one concern. The three main training topics, in order, were safety, courtesy, and cleanliness. Page seven warns, "Fire is our worst enemy"—a fitting statement but probably not practiced so much as it was preached, since a preventable fire on April 26, 1984, involving smoldering embers from a welder's torch in the Lost River ride likely caused the massive fire that ultimately led to Idora Park's permanent closure five months later. Firefighters were greatly hampered in their efforts when one of the two fire hydrants at the park did not provide sufficient water pressure, and the other was inoperable. (Hardy.)

Idora employed year-round full-time employees, year-round part-time employees, part-time summer employees, and contractors who were specialists in ride or attraction service and repair. In the 1975 photograph above, Wilbur Horvath, ride maintenance supervisor, looks up from his work. Horvath's office was in a building under the noisy Wildcat roller coaster. He walked the entire Wildcat track every day to inspect the ride for safety. Maybe the bottle of whiskey on his desk helped settle his nerves after those harrowing inspections or served as his personal reward for surviving it. The first-aid station (below) was located at the far northwest corner of the upper midway between the Heidelberg and the Funhouse. It was attended by nursing personnel. (Above, Toth; below, Mossman.)

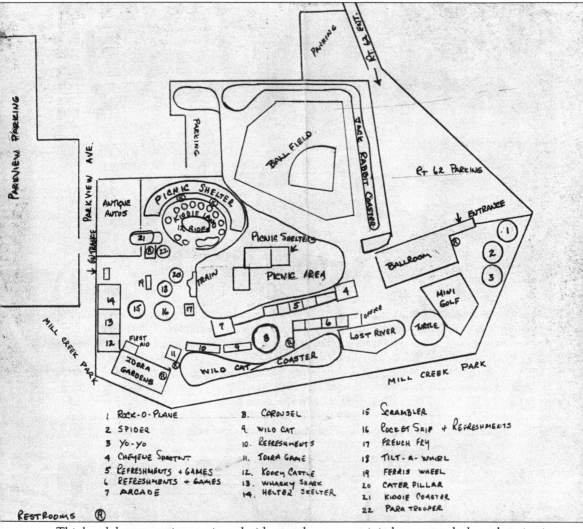

1 ROCK-O-PLANE	8. CAROUSEL	15 SCRAMBLER
2 SPIDER	9 WILD CAT	16 ROCKET SHIP + REFRESHMENTS
3 YO-YO	10. REFRESHMENTS	17 FRENCH FRY
4 CHEYENE SHOOTOUT	11. IDORA GAME	18 TILT-A-WHIRL
5 REFRESHMENTS + GAMES	12. KOOKY CASTLE	19 FERRIS WHEEL
6 REFRESHMENTS + GAMES	13. WHACKY SHARK	20 CATER PILLAR
7 ARCADE	14. HELTER SKELTER	21 KIDDIE COASTER
		22 PARA TROOPER

RESTROOMS ®

This hand-drawn map is not oriented with a north arrow, nor is it drawn to scale, but otherwise, it fairly accurately depicts the park in 1984. The map is oriented so that east is at the top and west is at the bottom. There were two main entrances to Idora Park. The entrance on Parkview Avenue is to the far left, and the entrance from Billingsgate Road to the parking lot is at the top, but is referred to here as Route 62 parking. Arriving from this parking lot, patrons would enter to the right, at the ballroom. The southernmost part of the midway shows the Rock-O-Plane, the Spider, and the Yo-Yo rides to the patrons' left upon entering. If arriving from Parkview Avenue, guests entered the northernmost part of the midway, with the Helter Skelter bumper car building to the immediate right and the Hooterville Highway farther away on the left. The building marked as Idora Gardens was actually the Crazy Horse Saloon in 1984. (MVHS.)

Two

FIRE, DEATH, AND DESTRUCTION

On April 26, 1984, fifteen fire company units with 37 firemen responded to a fire at Idora Park. The nearest fire hydrant was close by, but it was inoperable. Frustrated firemen ran hoses to the only other hydrant at the park, with the same result. The truck pumping units hit the fire with the water from their tanks while firemen searched for hydrants outside the park. (Reedy.)

The firemen believed that they were more than holding their own and were turning the corner on the fire, but hydrant water was still direly needed. A working hydrant or two could have put the finishing touches on the fire and saved more of the park's resources. Unfortunately, the pumper truck tanks ran dry before the fire could be extinguished. By the time hydrant water finally reached the hoses, the fire had regained strength, consuming more of the Lost River, and had jumped across to the Old Mill, engulfing it. It was too late to save the Lost River, the Wildcat, the park office, the entire west side of the lower midway, and a portion of the northeast end of the lower midway where the fire had jumped across. Even parts of the Turtle ride, farther south, were scorched. Fortunately, the carousel pavilion and the merry-go-round within it were kept doused with water and were saved. (TIPE.)

Prior to the fire, the Jack Rabbit had been reconfigured to run backward and had been renamed the Back Wabbit. The owners had hoped that the novelty of running the coaster backward would help increase attendance at the park because the number of park-goers had been steadily declining over the years, blamed in large part on the loss of many jobs when the steel mills closed. However, after the fire took the Wildcat and Lost River, nothing was going to save Idora, not even a backward running coaster. Note the guilty fire hydrant at left below, attempting to hide behind the lamppost. (Both, Mossman.)

Idora Park closed in September 1984 and held an on-site auction on October 20–21. Huge crowds attended both days. The very first items to be auctioned were a pair of tiki idols with shields that sold for $90. Some of the more interesting items included the Fish Pond and counter for $175, the Lost River sign for $55, the entire Kooky Castle for $2,000, and Laffin' Lena for $2,500. Her Loony Land brought $1,100. The lead horse of the merry-go-round sold for $17,500; another horse went for $20,500, and another went even higher at $23,000. After the bidding was completed, the total for all of the horses and the two chariots was determined, and the auctioneers rounded that figure up to ask for a bid of $385,000 for the entire merry-go-round. The Walentas from New York put forth the bid, and it was accepted. All 15 of the Wildcat coaster cars sold for $1,700. The white rabbit from Kiddieland mysteriously disappeared prior to the auction. (TIPE.)

112

In May 1986, a suspicious fire raged on the upper midway. A passing police patrol saw the fire and called it in. The fire appeared to have started somewhere near the Wildcat roller coaster, but brisk winds pushed it toward the upper midway. Fire crews arrived and fought the blaze but were unable to save the Heidelberg Gardens building, erected in 1899; the Funhouse, built in 1922; and the Helter Skelter bumper car building. Again, firefighters were hampered by a lack of working fire hydrants. One year earlier, Mount Calvary Pentecostal Church bought the property and vowed to build a "City of God" there. (Both, TIPE.)

Despite new ownership, Idora was falling farther into decay as the years went by. It appeared that the new owners had no intention of reviving the park. Several buildings and wooden coaster structures still stood, even after the 1984 and 1986 fires, but they were neglected and falling apart by the late 1980s. Vandals and treasure hunters frequently visited the property looking for adventure or a piece of Idora Park memorabilia. A baby grand piano, too large to steal, lay damaged inside the ballroom. A park cash register lay among the weeds, with its drawer pried out and missing. (Above, Zagorsky; left, McKinney.)

By 2001, a third fire had taken the ballroom, located just to the right of the still-standing Jack Rabbit roller coaster. Several groups had tried to save and revive the ballroom, but a suspicious fire ended those hopes. The Jack Rabbit met a similar fate in the summer of 2001, when it was demolished by an excavator. Luckily, the coaster cars were saved, and one of those is with The Idora Park Experience. The excavator also tore down the remains of the Wildcat. Idora's Famous French Fries building eventually collapsed and was hauled off as scrap. What was left of Idora Park was being erased. Two French fry holder boards were rescued and are at The Idora Park Experience. (Both, Zagorsky.)

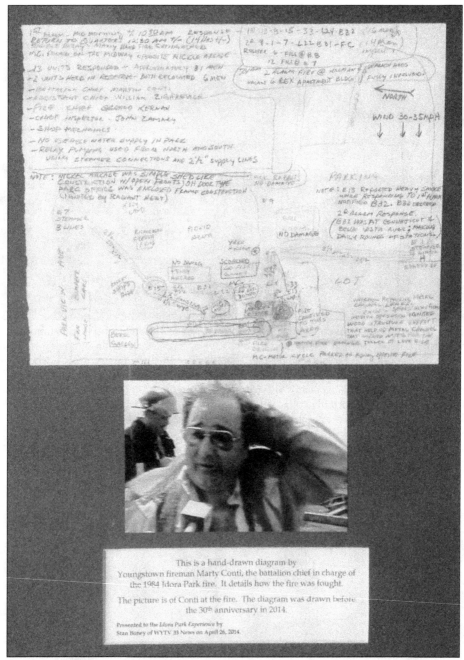

This is a hand-drawn diagram by
Youngstown fireman Marty Conti, the battalion chief in charge of
the 1984 Idora Park fire. It details how the fire was fought.

The picture is of Conti at the fire. The diagram was drawn before
the 30th anniversary in 2014.

Presented to the Idora Park Experience by
Stan Boney of WYTV 33 News on April 26, 2014.

For the 30th anniversary of the 1984 Idora Park fire, April 26, 2014, Stan Boney, then an anchor with WYTV Channel 33 News in Youngstown, interviewed Marty Conti, the battalion fire chief in charge at the 1984 fire. During the interview, Conti took out a scrap of paper and began writing notes and drawing a sketch from his recollection of the fire. Boney was surprised at Conti's memory and the accuracy of his notes and drawings of an event from 30 years earlier. Boney asked Conti if he could keep the paper, and Conti agreed. When The Idora Park Experience opened for the first time on the 30th anniversary of the fire, Boney surprised the authors with this framed presentation of the scrap of paper along with a photograph of Conti at the fire in 1984. (TIPE.)

Three

FROM OUT OF THE ASHES

The Idora Park Carousel—or merry-go-round, as it was commonly called when it was in Youngstown—was bought at the farewell auction in October 1984. The purchase price was $385,000. It was beautifully restored and now resides in a glass complex in an area of New York City known as DUMBO (Down Under Manhattan Bridge Overpass). (TIPE.)

R.E. Chambers built all of the rocket ships in Idora Park. The Idora Park Experience owns a Chambers rocket, but it is not from Idora. After three years of numerous requests to see Idora Park's rockets, a visit was finally agreed to by their owner in 2015. Unfortunately, Idora's rockets had spent the past 30 years outside rotting away (above) and were not permitted to come home to Ohio. The "last man standing" at the park was the stone water fountain that stood on the upper midway since Idora's earliest days. It got that name because every other manmade thing had been erased from the park. Deteriorating from neglect and vandalism, the fountain was donated to The Idora Park Experience and is awaiting restoration. (Above, TIPE; below, Reedy.)

The elusive white rabbit from Kiddieland was finally located, but its custodian was not willing to part with it because it had been a part of the family for 35 years. Attempts to purchase the white rabbit were made by letter and telephone, all to no avail. The rabbit had allegedly been stolen, then retrieved, then mysteriously disappeared again just prior to the auction in October 1984. A reliable source named the street where the white rabbit had been found after the first theft, which, coincidentally, is the same street where it currently sits. (TIPE.)

In 2012, an agreement was made to purchase the last standing Victorian-style lamppost, as seen above on the left, as well as the large green globe that remained above the Idora Park office. Author Jim Amey and several friends were able to lower and remove the lamppost with only slight damage. The green globe, seen below, was another matter. Before it could be removed, it was stolen. For 28 years after the park's closure, it had stood unmolested, but now it was gone. Two years later, on April 26, 1984, at the initial opening of The Idora Park Experience, a woman approached Amey and asked if he would be interested in an Idora Park artifact. A deal was made, and the green globe was purchased a second time. (Above, Nard; below, Garland.)

Small trinkets from the park, like an ashtray, a cigar box, a pendant here, and a poster there, were nice to have, but something big was needed. Several years ago, an anonymous caller informed author Jim Amey of an Ohio collector with "big stuff" from Idora Park. The collector's name was given, and after much cajoling, he agreed to meet. His name was Mike Pacak, and he truly did have big stuff from Idora Park. A trip was made, and an agreement was reached for the first big item from Idora Park. A Wildcat coaster car (above) exchanged hands. Minutes later, another big item was added—the rear Jack Rabbit coaster car. And this was just the beginning. (Both, Zagorsky.)

After years of placing advertisements in all the local newspapers as well as on the internet, a phone call came in from Bob Lisko. His father, Steve, had bought the Idora Park Tilt-A-Whirl and Caterpillar rides at the auction in 1984. The rides were no longer serviceable, so Lisko was willing to part with a few items. A deal was made, and one Tilt-A-Whirl car and three Caterpillar cars were purchased. Lisko then donated the original signs from both rides. The Idora Park Experience restored the Tilt-A-Whirl car and one of the Caterpillar cars. Thanks go to Carol and Dennis Singley, who posed for these photographs and also donated the snake prize (shown) that Dennis won for Carol at Idora Park in 1969. (Both, TIPE.)

The whereabouts of the three Baby Wildcat coaster cars was a mystery. The roller coaster and its cars were built at Idora Park in 1934, and the ride occupied three different locations in an effort to keep it near the other children's rides. The Baby Wildcat sold at auction for $800 but was never removed. It was abandoned and left to decay. In the 1990s, the three coaster cars were on display in the window of a closed shop in Lowellville, Ohio. By the time author Jim Amey learned of this, the cars were gone and did not appear again until 2014, when they were found on top of an ice-cream shop 100 miles away in West Virginia. A deal was made to purchase the three cars, and a crane was hired to retrieve them from the roof. All three cars are now on display at The Idora Park Experience. (TIPE.)

The Idora Park Experience was gaining momentum and credibility, as people witnessed the effort put forth in trying to save the memory of the park. A network was forming. Amusement park enthusiast Joe Cappello Jr. shared the whereabouts of a turtle from Idora Park's Turtle ride. Soon, a deal was made, and the Turtle was purchased. Above, artist Keith "Skeeter" Sturgeon paints the turtle's face after it was restored by the students at the Mahoning County Career and Technical Center (MCCTC). Below, student Josh Gionest and teacher Joe Sander of the MCCTC auto body collision course take on another restoration project: one of the Mercedes-Benz kiddie cars from Idora. A Hooterville Highway car was restored by MCCTC students in 2019. (Both, TIPE.)

Phil McLaughlin is a retired Navy man from Struthers, Ohio, living in Virginia. He spent much of his childhood at Idora. In 2014, he came to the museum to drop off a working model of the Rocket Ship ride that he built. After that came a working model of the French fry stand, then a working model of Laffin' Lena's Loony Land. A Rapids/Lost River boat followed, and after that, a model of the Billingsgate parking building. His latest creation is the *Idora Limited* train station. Below, Christine and Ray Kondas stand in front of the 18-foot scale model of the Wildcat roller coaster built by John Kondas, who passed away soon after building the model. It has since been purchased by The Idora Park Experience and is on display. (Both, TIPE.)

This train was made by the Miniature Train Company of North Tonawanda, New York, in 1950 with the designation Train No. 419. It was delivered to Idora Park in 1951 and remained until the park closed in 1984. It sold at the 1984 auction for $6,000. The authors paid considerably more for it 20 years later. Testing the train's load limit are, from left to right, Rick, Richard, Bob, Bill, and Jim Amey. After filling a corner of the museum with authentic Idora Park arcade machines, it seemed only fitting to build a mock-up of the exterior of the actual arcade for visitors. (Both, TIPE.)

Rumors of a Rapids/Lost River boat swirled for years but always resulted in a dead end. Armed with flyers with a photograph of a boat sent by an anonymous person, author Jim Amey went door to door looking for the elusive boat. The second house was that of Jack and Sally Kenney. As if by divine intervention, the boat was in their backyard. They had received it decades earlier from a neighbor, who at one time had owned all the surviving boats. The Kenneys happily donated the boat, but retrieving it was difficult thanks to a wasp infestation. Attempts to avoid or destroy the wasps only increased their attacks. Finally, the fragile boat was removed but damaged while avoiding wasp stings. The Kenneys are shown below in the restored Rapids/Lost River boat. (Above, TIPE; below, Kenney.)